Love and Unanswered Questions

Chase DeSalvo

Perfect Love

And our eyes met for the very first time,
for the very last.
I lived a lifetime within that glance.
It was the perfect connection with the perfect
stranger.
But there's no such thing as perfect love.

Forgiveness

I find it is easier to forgive others than it is to
forgive myself.
I find that I am no longer at peace.
No one speaks upon what to do when you've
broken one's own heart.
Forgiveness waits for no one,
and every day I'm late to the bus stop.

Fire and Ice

I am more of a book by the lake,
underneath the moonlight,
longing to see a shooting star,
type.

She's the fire that melts my ice,
and keeps me moving.
She's the energy that can't be matched,
one of a kind,
type.

I cannot resist.

Wrong Places

You know what the funny thing about love is?
People long for love so desperately.
A love where the atmosphere in the room
changes as soon as they walk in.
A love that serves as a safe house when it seems
as if the rest of the world is against you.
Love that makes you feel understood.
Makes you so terrified but only because you fear
losing that love.
People long for love that makes them feel
complete.
The funny thing about love is,
people are looking in the wrong places.
This love is only found inside of you.
You see,
true love is loving yourself.
It's loving all of your flaws,
all your little imperfections.
It's giving yourself space to sit with the pain and
the tears.
Loving yourself is sitting under the stars and
realizing that you were never incomplete to
begin with.
This love is within all of us,

buried beneath the million lies and thoughts we
have about ourselves.
Loving yourself isn't easy,
but it's the purest form of love we could ever
find.
And yes,
it will be worth it.

Killing my sorrows

Champagne invited me out for brunch.
So innocent I thought,
I'll oblige.
Whiskey found out and demanded a date.
Her and I have such a toxic relationship, but
once again I'll oblige.
Tequila slipped in through the back door of the
party.
She tells me she can help put my sorrows to bed.
I said, I'll drink to that.
However,
the next morning my sorrows were right there
next to me,
waiting on me to wake up.

Past, Present, Future

The past is where most people live.
 Happy memories, brutal regrets, every moment
turns into the past with every second that passes.
The past is all we really know.

The present is the loneliness.
No one really lives in the present.
The present is spent thinking of the past or the
future.
And yet, the present is all we really know.

The future is the scariest.
People want to dream the life they want so they
visit the future.
The future is for moving on.
All we do is work for the future.
The future is all we really know.

Ghosts

Ghosts of the person I used to be won't stop
haunting me.
They live inside of me,
begging me to be better.
But I think I've become one of them.

Black Hole

She's my black hole.
When I'm with her,
nothing else exists.
Time disappears.
She's like being in a whole new universe.
One where I can lay in her arms,
forever.

Thoughts I Had

You can't plan out your future.
Life just happens.
And sometimes you're the bad guy,
which makes you feel like you don't deserve
happiness or something better.
But you do,
the future can wait.

Potential

You can't fall in love with potential.
You will break your own heart.
You can't say, I can change them.
Everyone changes and gets better eventually.
But you have to learn to love them where they
are now,
the good and the bad.

The Dance

12

The dragonflies dance throughout the night sky,
for God has painted the sky pink tonight.
The piano from the lake house starts to play.
The waves crash against the dock in a gentle,
inviting way.
Now I'm dancing with them.

For Gravity

This one's for gravity.
For the way you make all things fall.
Like how pinecones and twigs fall on the front
porch,
Or how the sun falls below the horizon every
night,
The way I keep falling and she's always right
there to pick me up,
The first leaf to fall after summertime, the way
that there's not only highs but also lows in life.
You can't be surprised when things fall, that's
gravity.

Growing in the Dark

Humans are one of the very few species to grow
in the dark,
We don't always need a light at the end of the
tunnel.
Some even prefer the tunnel to have no light.
Not in a depressing matter,
but in a way that invites the unknown.
The ones you don't always need a plan for the
future.
I like to think of it as controlled chaos, it's like a
happy confusion.
Something that allows us to not only grow in the
dark, but thrive in the dark. Some say that the
light at the end of the tunnel means the fun is
over.
I know that's not true though.
Just a new chapter of life that we will all get to
one day.
Until then,
I will continue to dance my way into the dark,
unknown, exciting roller coaster of events we
call life.

Warmth

15

I stay up all night staring at the dying moon,
waiting for the sun to come alive.
And still,
only the thought of you warms me up.

October

Oh what a time.
I caught her sipping the moonlight right out of
the salty rim I gave her as a party gift that thirsty
October night.
Oh what a night.
I felt the ghost of her passing right through me
as we made eye contact on that back porch
Perfect weather.
If only I would have committed to something
and not have destroyed everything in my path.
Like some kind of serial killer.
Only in October.

What if

What if I leave here.
Then what?
Do I lose everything and everyone?
Do I lose us?
But what if I love it?
What if it's everything I've always wanted?
I once thought that was you.
And maybe it still is.
But maybe I'm not ready.
Will I ever be?
What if I stay?
Then what?

Love is a song

Sometimes I choke on the blood from my own
hands.
Then I listen to music.
I get lost in every lyric.
I feel seen in every beat of the drum.
I am no longer choking.
In fact, I am eager to walk into my next storm
with confidence.

My muse

She does not believe me when I tell her she's
beautiful.
I fear for the day when I mess up,
And she realizes her true beauty after all.

Dreams

In this dream,
I'm a movie star again.
I say again, but I never was one to begin with.

Some days, it feels like I always was a movie
star.
Born in a rich family with plenty of acting
lessons to attend to.

And some days I'm experiencing every day life
again.
No movie star.

Depends on which dream I decide to visit.
I could visit today as a memory.
I say memory but I never really will get the full
details and plus today wasn't very exciting.

So in this dream, I will be hope.
By which I mean that I will hope for rich parents
in the next life.

Some People

Some people wear their hearts on their sleeves.
Some people absolutely love others with all that
they have.

I barely have the energy to love myself with all
that I have.
I want to be there for everyone.
I do.
But I feel drained after taking care of myself.
Can this change?

Dandelion

My hope for you is that you find your dandelion.
You find your dandelion whom was once a seed
that was stolen by some unforgivable invisible
force of nature.
But thankfully was returned to you by the
universe and you were able to nurture them.
But once they return to you they have already
grown into an independent and fierce force.
One with enough beauty to freeze time.
One that does not need you.
But wants you.
This is the dandelion whom you deserve.